...enew by date shown.

kids' kitchen

fun recipes with a dash of science!

lorna brash

WAYLAND

First published in 2013 by Wayland
Copyright © Wayland 2013

Wayland
338 Euston Road
London NW1 3BH

Wayland Australia
Level 17/207
Kent Street
Sydney, NSW 2000

Editor: Debbie Foy
Designer: Lisa Peacock/Simon Daley
Photographer: Ian Garlick
Home economist: Lorna Brash
Consultant: Sean Connolly

Dewey: 641.5'123-dc23

ISBN 978 0 7502 7823 2

Printed in China

10 9 8 7 6 5 4 3 2 1

Wayland is a division of Hachette Children's Books,
an Hachette UK company.
www.hachette.co.uk

contents

ARE YOU HUNGRY TO LEARN MORE ABOUT YOUR FOOD?

Have you ever wondered why some foods behave the way they do? Have you ever looked closely at popcorn and wondered how your puffy, chewy snack started life as a hard yellow seed?

Or, have you ever bitten into a pizza and wondered how that rubbery ball of mozzarella has transformed into a stringy goo?

How do soggy egg whites combine into a crisp, white meringue? How can you bake ice cream in the oven? Or make delicious bread in a seedy flowerpot?

Find out the answers to these questions and more in **Kids' Kitchen!**

HAPPY ~~EXPERIMENTING~~ COOKING!

THE KITCHEN RULE BOOK

→ Always wash your hands before you start cooking and after handling raw meat

→ Mop up spills as soon as they happen

→ Use oven gloves for handling hot dishes straight from the oven

→ Take care with sharp knives. Don't walk around with them!

→ Switch off the oven or cooker top when you have finished cooking

→ Use separate chopping boards for vegetables and meat

→ Store raw and cooked foods separately in the fridge

→ Don't forget to tidy up the kitchen afterwards! No brainer, huh?

ABBREVIATIONS

g = grammes

tsp = teaspoon

tbsp = tablespoon

ml = millilitres

°C = degrees Celsius

HOT GOODS!

WHEN YOU SEE THIS WARNING SIGN AN ADULT'S HELP MAY BE NEEDED!

The 'Science Bits'

Believe it or not, cooking involves a lot of science! The Science Bits that accompany each of the delicious recipes answer all the mysteries about food that you have ever wondered about. They also explore some of the interesting, unusual or downright quirky ways that our food can often behave!

smashing snacks: the recipes

smashing

snacks

POP-TASTIC POPCORN

Have you ever wondered how a tiny, hard seed explodes to nearly **40** times its original size, and becomes a yummy snack? Sweet or salty popcorn is the perfect cinema treat, but our combination of spices leaves you with a really deliciously pop-tastic snack for any time of day!

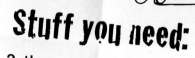

Stuff you need:

2 tbsp corn oil
75g popcorn kernels
15g salted butter
1 garlic clove, crushed
1 tsp curry powder
1/2 tsp mild chilli powder
1/4 tsp fine table salt

Serves 6

HOT GOODS!

Step 1

Place the oil into a medium-sized saucepan and heat until the oil is hot but not smoking.

Step 2

Add the popping corn and stir. Cover with a tight-fitting lid and place over a high heat, holding the lid firmly in place and shaking the pan occasionally. You will hear the corn pop!

Popcorn kernels have been known to pop up to 90cm into the air!

Step 3

In a separate pan, melt the butter until foaming, then add the garlic, curry and chilli powders and cook for 30 seconds, stirring with a wooden spoon.

The Science Bit

How does popcorn pop?

When the popcorn kernels are heated in the pan, the trapped moisture inside them expands and turns into steam. The build-up of steam is so intense that it bursts through the hard outer shell and the starch inside the kernel explodes, literally turning it inside out! The soft starch expands and puffs up to form the fluffy, yummy corn snack that we all love!

Step 4

Add the popped corn to the butter mixture and stir well. Turn it out into a bowl, sprinkle with salt and toss the popcorn with your hands until well mixed.

Stuff you need:

Non-stick Teflon mat
200g caster sugar
150g golden syrup
100g salted peanuts
50g shelled pistachio nuts,
roughly chopped
4 tbsp sesame seeds
1 tsp vanilla extract
25g softened butter
1 tsp bicarbonate of soda

Serves 6-8

HOT
GOODS!

The Science Bit

How does sugar become brittle, just like glass?

When sugar is heated the sugar crystals (that are arranged in the clever little 3D granules you can see in your sugar bowl) break down. As they cool, the sugar molecules join up, but they are no longer crystals. This means that light can now appear through the gaps in the molecules, making the shards transparent, and able to shatter, just like glass!

SMASHING CARAMEL SHARDS

These brittle shards of caramel with healthy nuts and seeds crackle and crunch in your mouth. Smash with a rolling pin and scatter over your favourite ice cream!

Step 1

Line a large baking sheet with a non-stick Teflon mat.

Step 2

Put the sugar, 60 ml water and golden syrup into a heavy based saucepan. Gently heat and stir until the sugar has dissolved. Bring to a gentle boil for **4-5** minutes until the mixture turns a pale toffee colour. Take care – the mixture will be very hot!

Step 3

Quickly add the nuts, seeds, vanilla, butter and bicarbonate of soda and blend until the butter has melted and the mixture is well combined.

Step 4

Quickly pour onto the non-stick mat. Leave to cool for at least 25 minutes before breaking into shards.

ICE CREAM IN A BAG!

Did you know that it's possible to make ice cream without a freezer? Follow our fun recipe to create delicious vanilla ice cream – all through the marvellous magic of science!

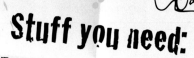

Stuff you need:

125ml whole milk
1 tbsp sugar
1/2 tsp vanilla extract
1x 500ml zip lock freezer bag
1x 900ml zip lock freezer bag
6 tbsp salt
21 ice cubes
A pair of woolly gloves!

Serves 1

Step 1

In a measuring jug, mix together the milk, sugar and vanilla, then pour the mixture into the 500ml zip lock bag and seal tightly. Set aside.

Step 2

Place the salt and ice cubes into the 900ml zip lock freezer bag. Place the smaller bag inside the larger one so that the two sealed edges are near each other.

Put on some pop music and dance as you shake your ice cream!

The Science Bit

How do you make ice cream without a freezer?

Easy-peasy! Salt lowers the freezing point of ice, causing it to melt. And when something melts, it absorbs heat energy from something else (in this case, the cream mixture). So, the cream loses heat (gets colder) until it begins to freeze. Shaking the bag stops it from freezing into one big block. Instead it creates tiny ice crystals in the milk fat, which in turn creates your deliciously creamy ice cream!

Step 3

Pop on your cosy gloves! Hold the two zip locked sealed edges together and

with both hands shake the bags for 8-10 minutes until you feel the milk mixture thicken to an ice cream.

Step 4

Remove the smaller bag from the larger bag. Wipe the bag to remove the salt (as you don't want salty ice cream - yuk!), but don't run it under the cold tap or your ice cream will melt. Squeeze the ice cream into a bowl, top with your favourite fruit and eat straight away!

Stuff you need:

25g butter, softened
2 slices brown bread
2 slices honey roast ham
75g mozzarella cheese, thinly sliced
1 ripe tomato, sliced
Basil leaves
Salt and black pepper

Serves 1

HOT GOODS!

The Science Bit

Why is mozzarella so stretchy?

Mozzarella is cool. You can bounce it like rubber, stretch it like elastic and melt it like plastic. Not many cheeses do all of that! When mozzarella is made, a mild acid (such as citric acid) is added to make the milk curdle. It is this combination of acid and heat that makes the texture of this cheese so stringy and elastic. The cheese curds are stretched and kneaded until smooth, and then they are formed into round balls as fresh mozzarella cheese!

CHEESE-AND-HAM-O-RAMA!

Crisp and toasty on the outside and **c**ooey-gooey cheese on the inside. Serve with green salad and a big dollop of ketchup for a finger-licking treat!

Step 1

Butter each slice of bread. Top one slice of bread with a piece of ham. Then add the mozzarella, sliced tomato and basil leaves. Season with salt and freshly ground black pepper. Finally add another slice of ham and then sandwich together with the remaining slice of bread.

Step 2

Preheat the grill to hot. Place the sandwich on a baking sheet and press to compact it slightly. Grill on the middle shelf for about 3 minutes or until the bread is golden.

Step 3

Carefully turn the sandwich over and grill for a further 3 minutes until bubbling and golden. Cut in half and serve.

HOMEMADE BEANS ON TOAST

Baked beans are often best known for their hilarious after-effects, but in fact they are packed full of protein, fibre, vitamins and minerals. If they are that good we thought we'd better find out how to make our own amazing version!

Stuff you need:

2 tbsp olive oil
2 red onions, finely chopped
150g streaky bacon, finely chopped
2 garlic cloves, crushed
1x 400g tin chopped tomatoes
2 tbsp dark muscovado sugar
1 tbsp Worcestershire sauce
2x 400g tins haricot beans
Salt and black pepper
4 slices crusty brown bread
1 tbsp butter
50g Cheddar cheese, coarsely grated

Serves 4

HOT GOODS!

Step 1

Add the oil to the saucepan and fry the onions and bacon for 8 minutes, stirring occasionally until softened. Add in the garlic, tomatoes, sugar and Worcestershire sauce. Bring to the boil, then reduce the heat to low, cover and cook for 20 minutes stirring occasionally until the sauce is thickened. Whizz with a hand blender until the sauce is thick.

Step 2

Drain the beans and stir them into the tomato sauce. Simmer for 5-10 minutes until warmed through. Season to taste with salt and freshly ground black pepper. Keep warm.

Step 3

Toast the bread until golden brown, and spread with butter. Spoon some of the beans over the toast. Sprinkle with grated cheese to serve.

The Science Bit

Why do beans give you wind?

It's simple. Beans are very high in fibre which is not easily broken down by our digestive systems. The partially broken down food passes further through the gut to the large intestine where it is further broken down creating carbon dioxide (CO_2) and other gases! We have used tinned beans in this recipe, but if you are using dried beans try soaking them overnight before cooking as this can help to break down the indigestible sugars that cause these noisy symptoms!

Stuff you need:

125g softened unsalted butter
125g caster sugar
1 egg
1 tsp vanilla extract
125g porridge oats
150g plain flour
½ tsp baking powder
125g white chocolate, chopped
125g plain dark chocolate, chopped

Makes 16 cookies

HOT GOODS!

These cookies are a great mid-morning snack as the oats fill up your tum for longer! Serve them with a fresh fruit berry smoothie.

Step 1

Preheat the oven to 180°C/fan 160°C/gas mark 4. Line two baking sheets with non-stick baking parchment. Beat the butter and caster sugar in a mixing bowl with a wooden spoon until creamy. Break in the egg and add the vanilla and oats and stir until mixed.

OAT-SO YUMMY POWER COOKIES

Step 2

Sift over the flour and baking powder and stir in the chopped chocolate until all the ingredients are well mixed together.

Step 3

Drop 16 teaspoonfuls of the cookie mixture evenly spaced apart onto the prepared baking sheets.

Step 4

Flatten slightly with the back of a fork. Bake for 12-15 minutes until risen slightly and golden. Transfer to a cooling rack to cool completely. Store in an airtight tin and eat within 1 week.

The Science Bit

Why are oats so good to eat in the morning?

Oats contain bags of fibre which adds bulk to your digestive system and slows down the digestive process. The body breaks down and burns fibre a lot slower than it does most other foods, so this makes you feel fuller for longer. The equation is: Feeling Full + Fewer Snacks = Healthier Diet!

'NO-CRY' ONION BHAJIS & DIP

Try these utterly spice-tastic 'no-cry' onion bhajis for a light and scrummy snack. Goggles are an unusual ingredient here...!

Step 1

For the dip, finely chop the cucumber and tomatoes. Stir both into the yogurt along with the fresh coriander. Season with salt and pepper.

Step 2

Place the gram flour, chilli powder, turmeric, ground coriander, cumin and salt into a large mixing bowl. Gradually whisk in 300ml water to make a smooth thick batter. Now pop on your goggles! Slice the onions and separate into rings.

Stuff you need:

For the dip:
4-cm piece cucumber
2 tomatoes
150ml Greek yogurt
Fresh coriander, chopped
Salt and black pepper

For the bhajis:
250g gram flour
1 tsp mild chilli powder
1 tsp ground turmeric
1 tsp ground coriander
1 tsp ground cumin
1/2 tsp salt
A pair of goggles
3 large Spanish onions
Sunflower oil, for frying

Serves 4

goggles

Onions ARE thought to Act AS An Anti-inflammatory, And So ARE often used to Soothe insect stings!

Step 3

Place the individual onion rings into the batter and stir well until all the onions are covered in batter.

Step 4

HOT GOODS!

Pour 2cm of oil into a deep frying pan and heat until a piece of bread turns golden in 20 seconds. Place spoonfuls of the onion mixture into the oil and cook for 3 minutes, turning half way through, until crispy and golden. Remove with a slotted spoon and drain on kitchen paper. Serve with the cool yogurt dip!

The Science Bit

Why do onions make you cry?

When you slice through an onion, sulphenic acids are released which mix with enzymes in the onion to produce a gas. This gas combines with the tears in your eyes to create a mild form of sulphuric acid, which irritates the surface of the eye. The eye's defence mechanism is to produce tears to wash away the irritation, but by wearing goggles, you are preventing the gas from getting into your eyes and making you cry!

DOUBLE-DIPPED MALLOW COOKIES

Do you like maths? Here's a simple sum for you: fluffy marshmallows + plain biscuits + chocolate + toasted coconut = cookie heaven!

Step 1

Place **4** pink marshmallows into the centre of **4** of the digestive biscuits and **4** white marshmallows into the centre of another **4** biscuits. Place one biscuit and mallow onto a plate and heat in a microwave for about **10** seconds. You will see the marshmallow 'explode' and double in size.

Step 2

Immediately use one of the plain digestives to make a 'sandwich' by pressing the two biscuits together gently. Set aside and cook the remaining biscuits and marshmallows until you have 8 cookie sandwiches.

Step 3

Break the chocolate into pieces, place it in a heatproof bowl and allow to melt over a saucepan of simmering water. Carefully remove the bowl from the saucepan. Place the chocolate into one dish and the coconut into another. Half dip the cookies into the chocolate and then the toasted coconut.

Step 4

Place the cookies on a baking tray lined with baking parchment. Allow to set completely. Store in an airtight tin.

The Science Bit

Can chocolate really make us feel good?

Of course chocolate makes us feel good, right? But in fact, recent scientific research has actually proved it! Apparently, eating chocolate can cause the brain to release endorphins which are chemicals that circulate in our blood to make us feel great! How cool is that? Bring on the choccy!

MINI SUPERHERO PIES!

These crisp mini pies are filled with tangy feta cheese, 'superfood' spinach and deliciously crunchy pine nuts. A great combination of healthy stuff with a tantalizing texture!

Stuff you need:

200g baby spinach leaves
150g feta cheese, crumbled
4 tbsp toasted pine nuts
Handful chopped mint and parsley
2 tbsp beaten egg
Salt and black pepper
270g filo pastry sheets
50g butter, melted

Makes 18 pies

HOT GOODS!

Step 1

Preheat the oven to 190°C/fan 170°C /gas mark 5. Wash the spinach and drain any excess water. Put it in a saucepan with only the water that is clinging to the leaves and place over a low heat until the spinach has wilted. Allow to cool.

Step 2

Stir the cheese, pine nuts, mint, parsley and beaten egg into the spinach and stir well to combine. Season with salt and black pepper.

Step 3

Cut the filo pastry sheets lengthways into three long, thin strips of an equal size. Cover two bundles of pastry strips with a clean tea towel to prevent them from drying out. Lift off two thin strips of filo pastry and brush each of them with melted butter. Cover each with another (unbuttered) pastry strip.

Step 4

Place a teaspoonful of the spinach filling at the bottom of the pastry strip. Lift the bottom right corner over the spinach to produce a triangle shape. Continue to flip the filled triangle over to create a triangular shape down the length of the filo strip. Repeat until you have used all the butter, pastry and spinach filling.

Step 5

Brush the mini pies with butter and bake for 20 minutes until golden brown.

The Science Bit

Do pine nuts come from pine trees?

Believe it or not, yes! Pine nuts are an edible seed that are found inside pine cones. They are also the main ingredient of pesto sauce. They have a high fat content and so to bring out their flavour it's a good idea to 'toast' them in a frying pan without oil.

GOLD BULLION HONEYCOMB BARS!

These bullion bars packed with crunchy honeycomb are pure gold (well, almost!). Keep them locked up in an airtight treasure chest (or tupperware container) or they won't be around for long!

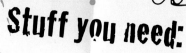

Stuff you need:

300g plain dark chocolate
300g unsalted butter
50g shelled, chopped hazelnuts
80g honeycomb chocolate bars, roughly crushed
100g digestive biscuits, broken into small pieces
50g raisins
Edible gold glitter

Makes 8 bars

HOT GOODS!

Step 1

Wet the insides of 8 mini loaf tins (or an 20-cm square cake tin if you don't have the mini version) with water. Then line the base and sides of the tins with clingfilm.

Step 2

Break the chocolate into squares and place in a heatproof bowl with the butter. Melt over a pan of simmering water until nice and runny. Then carefully remove the bowl from the heat.

Step 3

Stir the hazelnuts, crushed honeycomb bars, biscuits and raisins into the runny chocolate. Fill

each tin with the mixture and level the surface. Leave to chill in the fridge for 45 minutes.

Step 4

Turn the chocolate mixture out of the tins by giving them a hard knock on a work surface. Remove the clingfilm. Wrap each bullion bar in gold paper and dust with edible gold glitter!

The Science Bit

Who or what is responsible for the holes in honeycomb?

Well, first off, the honeycomb that we've used in this recipe needs really high heat to make, which is why we have used shop-bought bars, but it is worth looking a little more closely at honeycomb with its wholly holey texture...
When bicarbonate of soda (an ingredient that helps mixtures rise) is heated with sugar syrup, oodles of carbon dioxide (CO_2) gas is released. It is this CO_2 that permeates the sugar mixture, creating the lovely bubbly melt-on-your-tongue texture of honeycomb!

Stuff you need:

4 unwaxed lemons
250g golden caster sugar
Large handful crushed ice
75g fresh raspberries
50g citric acid (available from pharmacy shops)
15g bicarbonate of soda
100g icing sugar

Serves 4-6

Different chemical taste detectors on parts of your tongue are programmed to detect the acidity of the sour lemons or the sweetness of the sugar!

The Science Bit

So what makes the fizz?

The bicarbonate of soda reacts with the acid in the lemons and the sugar to form carbon dioxide (CO_2) gas. This gas is released in millions of small fizzy bubbles which rise to the surface of the lemonade to try to escape!

PINK FIZZBOMB LEMONADE

Try this fruity and refreshing drink with a cool tongue-tingling effect as the bubbles get busy!

Step 1

Cut each lemon into about 8 wedges. Remove any pips and place into a food processor or blender. Add half the sugar, the crushed ice and 500ml water. Blend to a puree.

Step 2

Place a sieve over a large bowl and pour the lemon mixture in. Sieve to remove the pith. Take the pith back to the food processor with the remaining sugar, raspberries and another 500ml water and whizz again. Sieve into the previous lemon mixture. Discard anything left in the sieve.

Step 3

Mix together the citric acid, bicarbonate of soda and icing sugar. Place a heaped teaspoonful into the bottom of a glass and pour over the lemon mixture. Give it a good stir and drink.

29

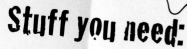

Stuff you need:

For the breadsticks:
175g strong plain bread flour, plus extra for dusting
1/2 tsp caster sugar
1/2 tsp coarse sea salt
1/2 tsp fast-action dried yeast
2 tbsp olive oil, plus extra for oiling

For the dip:
2 tbsp soured cream
2 tbsp mayonnaise
50g Cheddar cheese, coarsely grated
1 spring onion, finely chopped
Pinch of cayenne pepper

Makes 12 breadsticks
(and enough dip for
4 people)

HOT GOODS!

What makes all those tiny holes in bread? Has something been eating it before you? Yeast is the stuff that makes bread rise – but what is it ? And how does it work?

Step 1

Mix the flour, sugar, salt and yeast into a large bowl. Make a well in the centre and pour in the olive oil and 100ml water (make sure the water is not boiling, just hand hot). Mix to a soft dough.

BIG DIPPER BREADSTICKS

Step 2

Knead the dough for for 8-10 minutes until it is smooth and elastic. Oil your mixing bowl and place the dough back into the bowl. Cover with a clean tea towel and leave to rise for 10 minutes.

Step 3

Cut the dough into 12 equal pieces and roll each into a long thin, stick about 25cm long. Sprinkle a little flour over two baking sheets and arrange the breadsticks evenly on the baking sheets. Leave to rise in a warm place for 45 minutes until doubled in size.

Step 4

Preheat the oven to 200°C/fan 180°C /gas mark 6. Bake the breadsticks for 18-20 minutes until golden. Mix together all the dip ingredients until well combined. Spoon into a bowl and dip in!

The Science Bit

What is yeast and how does it work?

Believe it or not yeast is a living fungi that converts the natural sugars in flour into carbon dioxide (CO_2). This gas is the cause of all the tiny little bubbles you can see in bread! Without yeast our bread would be hard and flat. With yeast, and a small amount of sugar for it to feed on, warmth and a good kneading, your homemade bread (or breadsticks) will have a delicious, soft texture.

dynamite dinners: the recipes

dynamite dinners

STICKY CHICKY BURGER STACKS

Everybody loves a burger! And good, wholesome burgers are made from good quality minced meat. But what is it that gives the burger its shape and what stops it from falling apart on your barbecue or grill? Read on...

HOT GOODS!

Step 1

In a large bowl mix together the minced chicken, soy sauce, chilli dipping sauce, lemon rind and juice and spring onions. Season with salt and freshly ground black pepper. Next, get your hands into the mixture and give it a good squeeze until all the ingredients are thoroughly combined.

Step 2

Divide the mixture into 8 equal-sized balls, then flatten them slightly so that you have 8 mini burgers. Place on a baking tray lined with foil.

Step 3

Preheat the grill to hot. Cook the burgers under the grill for 7-8 minutes on each side until cooked through. While the burgers are cooking, split the rolls and tear the lettuce leaves in half. Place one torn lettuce leaf over 8 halves of the rolls. Top with the sliced tomatoes. Place the cooked burgers over the top then add the bread roll lids. Serve with homemade mayonnaise or ketchup (page **14-15**).

The Science Bit

What holds your burger together?

The stuff that stops your burger (as well as people and most animals!) falling apart is a protein called collagen. Minced meat contains collagen and when it is cooked with a liquid (in this case soy sauce) the collagen is broken down into a softer substance called gelatine (used to make jelly!).

This binds the minced meat together and helps your burger to keep its yummy, burger-y shape!

The Science Bit

Why does peeled avocado quickly turn brown?

Avocados (and lots of other fruits) turn brown when exposed to air because of a chemical reaction known as oxidation. But we can help to stop this reaction with a squeeze of lemon juice! Why? Because vitamin C in the lemon juice (called ascorbic acid) slows down the oxidation process and helps the avocado to stay fresh and green for longer!

Stuff you need:

4 large soft flour tortillas
2 tbsp olive oil
1 little gem lettuce
100g cherry tomatoes, halved
1/4 cucumber, finely chopped
400g tinned mixed bean salad, drained
200g sweetcorn kernels
1 avocado, cut into chunks and tossed with 2 tbsp lemon juice
4 tbsp vinaigrette dressing
50g Cheddar cheese, grated

Serves 4

Avocados have the highest protein content of any fruit!

TEX-MEX TACO BOWL SALAD

Make your own edible taco bowl to serve this delicious salad! Work quickly with the avocado to keep it looking fresh and green – add it at the end and serve immediately.

Step 1

Preheat the oven to 180°C/fan 160°C/gas mark 4. Brush the tortillas with oil on both sides and place in heatproof bowls, shaping the sides to make a 'taco bowl'. Bake for 8–9 minutes until crisp and set into a bowl shape. Allow the taco bowls to cool completely before removing.

Step 2

Shred the lettuce and toss with the tomatoes, cucumber, beans, sweetcorn, avocado with lemon juice and dressing. Spoon the salad into the taco bowls.

Step 3

Finally, scatter the grated cheese over the top and serve!

INCREDIBLE EDIBLE BOWL SOUP!

Here's an amazing fish soup which allows you to eat the bowl AND its contents! And while we're at it, let's have a look at how the haddock gets its lovely smoky flavour...

Step 1

Preheat the oven to 200°C/fan 180°C /gas mark 6. Pinch a 'lid' from the top of the bread roll and set aside. Then scoop out the soft bread from inside leaving a 1/2-inch layer of bread inside.

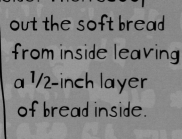

Stuff you need:

6 crusty cob bread rolls
1-2 tbsp olive oil
500g potatoes, peeled
1 large onion, peeled
1.2 litres milk
1 garlic clove, crushed
300g tinned sweetcorn with red pepper, drained
450g smoked haddock fillets, skinned
Salt and black pepper
Handful flat-leaf parsley, chopped

Serves 6

HOT GOODS!

When you toast a slice of bread a chemical reaction occurs that alters the sugars and proteins in the bread!

Step 2

Brush the insides of the rolls with oil and bake for 15 minutes until golden. This will 'seal' the inside of the roll. Chop the potatoes and onion into small chunks and place in a large saucepan.

Step 3

Add the milk to the potatoes and onion and bring to the boil. Turn down the heat, cover and simmer for 10 minutes.

Step 4

Next, stir in the garlic, sweetcorn mixture and fish. Bring back to the boil, then turn down the heat, cover and simmer for 5 minutes until the fish flakes easily with a fork. Season to taste with salt and pepper. Stir in the parsley.

Step 5

Spoon the soup into the bread rolls and serve (and eat!) immediately.

The Science Bit

Why do we smoke fish?

Before fridges were invented freshly caught fish was preserved by smoking it over slow burning wood chips to stop it from rotting. Smoking absorbs moisture from the fish and inhibits the growth of bacteria which can cause it to decay. Smoking also stops fat on the surface of the fish 'going off' (due to oxidation), and so protects the inside of the fish, which is good to eat!

POSH FISH 'N' CHIPS 'N' DIP!

A fish and chip supper is a yummy treat – and one that might even help to make you a bit brainier…!

HOT GOODS!

Step 1

Preheat the oven to 200°C/fan 180°C/gas mark 6. Cut the potatoes lengthways into wedges and toss with

the olive oil. Spread into a single layer on a baking sheet, sprinkle with salt and pepper and roast for 30–35 minutes until crisp and golden.

Step 2

To make the dip, finely chop the watercress and stir into the mayonnaise. Add the gherkins. Chill until ready to use.

Step 3

Place the flour, the eggs and the breadcrumbs (mixed with the cayenne pepper) into three separate dishes. First, dip the fish into the flour to coat, then into the egg and finally into the breadcrumbs to coat evenly.

Step 4

Pour about 2cm of oil into a deep frying pan and heat until a piece of bread turns golden in 30 seconds. Cook the fish in batches for 2-3 minutes until crisp and golden. Drain on kitchen paper and keep warm while cooking the remaining fish. Serve hot with the chips and the gherkin mayo dip.

The Science Bit

Does eating fish really make you brainy?

You've heard this loads of times, right? Well, while eating fish won't instantly make your maths homework easier, scientists believe there is some truth to it. The 'magic' ingredient in fish is omega-3 fatty acids which are found in all fish but mainly in 'oily' fish such as fresh tuna, mackerel, sardines, herring and salmon!

PIMP YOUR BURGER!

Ketchup-at-home

What's thick and red and great with chips? Yep, it's tomato ketchup. Make your own super homemade version to serve with Sticky Chicky Burger Stacks (page 6).

Step 1

Place all the ingredients except the sugar into a food processor and whizz to a smooth puree.

Step 2

Pour the puree into a pan and bring to the boil. Sprinkle over the sugar and stir until dissolved. Reduce the heat and simmer for 30 minutes, stirring until thickened. Allow to cool for 5–10 minutes.

Step 3

Decant the ketchup into a clean container. Seal and store in the fridge. Use within 3 weeks once opened.

Stuff you need:

400g tomato puree
225ml cider vinegar
2 onions, peeled and finely chopped
1 large potato, peeled and diced
50g fresh root ginger, peeled and finely grated
2 sticks celery, finely chopped
3 garlic cloves, crushed
1 tsp ground cinnamon
1 tsp ground cloves
2 tsp fine table salt
1 tsp freshly ground black pepper
125g muscovado sugar

Makes 600ml

HOT GOODS!

Homemade Mayo

Q: How do two liquids combine together to make a yummy, thick and creamy mayonnaise?

A: See 'The Science Bit' for an explanantion of this kitchen magic!

Stuff you need:

2 egg yolks
1/2 tsp salt
1/2 tsp Dijon mustard
2 tbsp white wine vinegar
250ml vegetable oil
Sauces or herbs

Makes 350ml

Step 1

Whisk the egg yolks, salt, mustard and vinegar with an electric whisk until well combined. Add the oil a spoonful at a time and whisk until the mixture starts to thicken. Continue until all of the oil has been used.

Step 2

Flavour up your mayo with 1-2 tbsp barbecue sauce, tomato ketchup or a small handful of chopped herbs, spring onions or chives.

The Science Bit

How do two liquids combine to make a solid?

Mayo is made from two main ingredients: vinegar and oil. If you shimmy and shake the two together in a jar, then leave them, after a while they will separate back out into oil and vinegar. However, if you add egg yolks, which contain fats, this stabilizes (or emulsifies) the mixture preventing the oil and vinegar separating and creating a yummy concoction to spread on your burger!

FINGER LICKIN' CHICKEN SATAY

You'll be licking your lips as well as your fingers with these marinated chicken sticks dipped in a perfectly peanutty sauce. It's a promise!

Step 1

Place the bamboo skewers in a shallow dish and spread them into a single layer. Pour cold water over them to cover. Leave for at least 30 minutes to soak.

Stuff you need:

12 bamboo skewers
500g boneless skinless chicken breasts
4 tbsp soy sauce
1 tbsp runny honey
1 tsp minced ginger
1 tsp minced garlic
Small handful fresh chopped coriander
4 tbsp crunchy peanut butter
3 tbsp sweet chilli dipping sauce
Lemon wedges, to serve

Makes 12 skewers

HOT GOODS!

Kitchen ALErt! Wash your hands AFTER handling RAW chicken

Step 2

Cut the chicken into chunks and place in a bowl with 2 tbsp of the soy sauce, honey, minced ginger, garlic and coriander. Give all the ingredients a good mix. Cover and set aside for 30 minutes.

Step 3

Remove the skewers from the water. Thread the chicken pieces onto the skewers and place on a baking tray. Cook them under a hot grill for 4-5 minutes on each side until golden brown.

Step 4

Place the peanut butter, remaining soy sauce, sweet chilli sauce and 90ml water into a saucepan and heat gently until smooth and thick. Serve the satay sticks with the peanut sauce and a squeeze of fresh lemon.

The Science Bit

Can I make healthier peanut butter at home?

Yes you can! Just whizz up 500g unsalted shelled peanuts, 2 tbsp peanut oil and a pinch of salt in a food processor. Keep it in a sealed container in the fridge and use within two weeks. The homemade stuff avoids using sweeteners and preservatives which help to prolong the shelf life of shop-bought peanut butter. Overall, your homemade version is much healthier!

JAPAN-EASY TUNA ROLLS

Made with one of the staple ingredients of Japanese food, sticky white rice, these sushi rolls are easy to eat – even with chopsticks!

Step 1

Wash the rice under the cold tap until the water runs clear. Place into a saucepan and add 475ml cold water. Bring the rice to the boil, then cover, reduce the heat and simmer for 15 minutes. Do NOT lift the lid. Leave the rice to stand for 10 minutes, then stir in the rice vinegar.

Stuff you need:

400g sushi rice (often called 'sticky rice')
6 tbsp rice wine vinegar
3 nori (dried seaweed) sheets
85g tinned tuna, drained and flaked
2 tsp mayonnaise
1/2 pimento, deseeded and cut into strips
1/4 cucumber, halved lengthways, deseeded and cut into sticks
Soy sauce, to serve

Serves 4

HOT GOODS!

Step 2

Place a piece of clingfilm a little larger than the nori sheet onto a work surface. Place the nori sheet on top. Spoon a third of the cooked rice into the centre of the nori sheet and spread to the edges leaving a 2-cm space along one edge of the nori.

46

Step 3

Mix the tuna and mayo and spread a third of it across the centre of the rice. Arrange a third of the pimento and cucumber sticks along the centre of the tuna mixture.

Step 4

Use the clingfilm to help you roll up the nori. The uncovered strip of nori will make a good 'seal' to the end of your sushi roll. Repeat with the remaining ingredients to make two more rolls.

Step 5

Unwrap the rolls and cut each into 5 equal-sized pieces. Dip your sushi pieces into soy sauce, eat and enjoy!

The Science Bit

Why is sushi rice so super-sticky?

It's the starch in rice that makes it so sticky. When you cook this short-grain rice, the water and heat soak into the grain and the starch molecules break down and absorb water to form a sticky 'gel' (this process is called gelatinization). Sushi rice is cooked using the absorption method which means no water remains after cooking. So the starch released into the water is then readily gobbled back up by the rice grain making it super-sticky!

Wow! Rice husks are so tough that in some countries they are used to make concrete!

TONGUE-TINGLING SWEET AND SOUR NOODLES

Get your taste buds a-jangling with this noodle dish that combines a range of flavours to really tantalize your tongue!

Step 1

Heat the oil in a wok or large frying pan and fry the onion for 3-4 minutes. Stir in the garlic, mushrooms, red pepper and carrot and stir-fry for 3 minutes more.

Stuff you need:

1 tbsp sunflower oil
1 small onion, chopped
1 garlic clove, crushed
140g button mushrooms, sliced
1 red pepper, deseeded and thinly sliced
1 carrot, peeled and cut into sticks
227g tin pineapple chunks in natural juice
1 tbsp cornflour
Juice of 1 lemon
2 tbsp tomato puree
3 tbsp soy sauce
125g egg noodles
2 spring onions, trimmed and sliced

Serves 4

HOT GOODS!

Step 2

Drain the pineapple chunks reserving the juice in a measuring jug. Add enough cold water to the pineapple juice to make 200ml of liquid. Add the pineapple to the stir-fry mixture and cook for 2-3 minutes, stirring occasionally.

Step 3

Meanwhile, mix the cornflour with the lemon juice to form a smooth white paste. Stir in the tomato puree, soy sauce and pineapple juice liquid.

Step 4

Cook the noodles in a pan of lightly salted boiling water according to the packet instructions. This should take about 3-4 minutes.

Step 5

Add the noodles to the stir-fry mixture and pour over the sauce. Turn up the heat and cook for 1-2 minutes, stirring until the sauce has become thick and glossy, coating all the ingredients. Scatter with the onions, then eat with chopsticks if you can!

The Science Bit

Can you taste sweet <u>and</u> sour?

Your tongue is covered with tiny little taste sensors called papillae. These detect the molecules in your food that gives it flavour. Scientists believe that we can detect five different flavours with our papillae. These are sweet, sour, salt, bitter and umami, which is a highly savoury, meaty flavour found in such foods as tomatoes and cured meat.

THIRSTY COUSCOUS CAKES!

Couscous is a North African food that is traditionally steamed and served with rich stews. The tiny couscous granules soak up boiling water as if by magic!

Stuff you need:

50g couscous
Large handful fresh coriander, finely chopped
1 small garlic clove, crushed
3 tbsp olive oil
1/2 tsp ground cumin
1/2 tsp ground coriander
2 tbsp pine nuts, toasted
50g feta cheese, finely diced
2 medium eggs, beaten
150g fine white breadcrumbs
Salt and black pepper
2 tbsp plain flour
4 tbsp sunflower oil, for shallow frying

Serves 4

HOT GOODS!

Step 1

Place the couscous in a large bowl and cover with 100ml of boiling water. Leave to stand for 10 minutes, then fluff up with a fork.

Step 2

Place the fresh coriander, garlic, oil, cumin and ground coriander into a food processor and whizz to a thick puree. Stir into the couscous with the pine nuts, feta cheese, half the beaten egg and half the breadcrumbs until well combined. Season with salt and pepper. Roll into 8 small balls and then flatten into burger shapes.

Step 3

Put the flour, the remaining egg and the remaining breadcrumbs into separate dishes (as shown). Dip the couscous cakes into the flour to cover, then into the beaten egg and finally the breadcrumbs to coat.

Step 4

Heat the oil in a frying pan. Carefully cook the couscous cakes in batches for 3 minutes on each side until golden. Serve with salad and homemade mayonnaise (see page 15).

The Science Bit

Why does couscous grow?

Couscous is granules of semolina made from durum wheat (the same stuff that pasta is made from). Durum wheat is high in gluten, a type of protein. The Latin word gluten means 'glue', and that gives us a clue as to why couscous grows, as it attracts and absorbs liquids. When you pour boiling water over the couscous, each granule can absorb its own volume in water, which makes it double in size!

SCRAMBLY EGG FRIED RICE

This is a totally dynamite dinner recipe that you can make so quickly and easily! Apart from the juicy chicken and vegetables, the little egg-coated grains of rice are what makes it oh-so special. So, come on, eggs – tell us how you do it!

Stuff you need:

350g long-grain rice
2 tbsp groundnut oil
2 garlic cloves, crushed
450g skinless chicken breasts, chopped
1 red pepper, deseeded and chopped
1 tbsp curry powder
1 bunch spring onions, thinly sliced
75g frozen peas, defrosted
2 tbsp light soy sauce
2 eggs, lightly whisked
Small handful fresh coriander, chopped

Serves 4

HOT GOODS!

The Science Bit

Why do eggs scramble?

Egg is a protein which changes instantly when heat is added. Proteins are made up of long chains of amino acids. When you whisk the white and yolk of an egg together you are creating new chemical bonds between the proteins in the egg white and the proteins in the yolk. Water from the yolk is trapped along with air, which was added when you whisked the eggs. Once heat is added the proteins clump together. If unstirred they form an omelette, but if stirred they form scrambled eggs as you are breaking down the protein connections.

Step 1

Bring a large pan of lightly salted water to the boil. Add the rice and stir with a wooden spoon. Cook for 12-15 minutes. Carefully lift the saucepan and pour the rice into a sieve.

Step 2

Pour the oil into a deep frying pan or wok. Heat gently then add the garlic, chicken and pepper and stir-fry for 8-10 minutes. Add the curry powder and cook for 1 minute.

Step 3

Add the cooked rice, spring onions and peas and cook for 5 minutes, stirring occasionally to make sure the ingredients do not stick. Drizzle over the soy sauce.

Step 4

Push the rice mixture to one side of the pan. Pour the eggs into the uncovered part and stir until they scramble, then mix with the rice. Scatter with coriander and serve!

SUPERFOOD CANNELLONI

Bright green spinach is a superhero's staple food as it's jam-packed to the brim with vitamins A and C, plus iron, zinc and potassium. Go get some on your plate!

HOT GOODS!

Step 1

Rinse the spinach well and place in a large saucepan. Heat gently, stirring, until the spinach starts to wilt. Sieve out any excess liquid, then add a pinch of nutmeg.

Step 2

Lay the lasagne sheets out on a work surface and spread with the cream cheese to cover. Lay the wilted spinach over the cream cheese.

Step 3

Roll up the lasagne sheets from the short end and place in a large ovenproof dish (large enough so that the lasagne rolls are in a single layer).

Step 4

Preheat the oven to 180°C/fan 160°C/gas mark 4. Heat the oil in a large saucepan and fry the onion, garlic and red pepper until softened. Stir in the tomatoes, tomato puree, herbs, passata and stock. Bring to the boil, cover and simmer for 20 minutes.

Step 5

Season with salt and pepper and then pour over the cannelloni rolls. Scatter over the cheese and bake for 30 minutes until bubbling. Garnish with basil leaves and serve with lots of green salad.

The Science Bit

Why is spinach so good for you?

Spinach is known as a superfood. It is low in calories and packed full of vitamins and minerals. To improve our body's absorption of iron from the spinach, it should be eaten with a source of vitamin C. So, squeeze fresh lemon juice onto cooked spinach before you eat it, or eat your superfood cannelloni with a large glass of fresh orange juice!

Stuff you need:

2 tbsp sunflower oil
500g lean minced beef
2 large onions, peeled and chopped
2 garlic cloves, crushed
1 tsp each ground cumin, coriander and oregano
1 tbsp mild chilli powder
1 red pepper, deseeded and chopped
125g chestnut mushrooms, sliced
2x 400g tins kidney beans, drained
2x 400g tins chopped tomatoes
2 tbsp tomato puree
2 tsp Worcestershire sauce
25g dark plain chocolate, finely chopped
Salt and black pepper

Serves 6

HOT
GOODS!

The Science Bit

Chillies and chocolate?

You may think the idea of putting chocolate and chillies together a bit weird, but the Mexicans have long since added chocolate to their 'mole' (sauces). As a fresh red chilli dries it develops a sweet, fruity flavour which, when combined with chocolate, makes an awesome combination. It is also thought that the richness of the melted chocolate helps to tone down some of the heat from the chilli.

CHILLI WITH A DEEP, DARK SECRET

A big hurrah for chilli — served with jacket potato, fluffy rice or any which way. But do you know the secret ingredient that Mexicans add to make the sauce truly rich and creamy?

Step 1

Heat the oil in a large pan and fry the minced beef for 5-6 minutes, stirring occasionally until browned all over.

Step 2

Add the onions and garlic and stir well. Cook for 3-4 minutes stirring now and then. Add the cumin, coriander, oregano and chilli powder and cook for 1-2 minutes. Don't allow the mixture to stick to the bottom of the pan.

Step 3

Add the remaining ingredients and bring to the boil. Season with salt and pepper. Cover and simmer gently for 45 minutes, stirring occasionally. Serve with rice or jacket potato.

mind-blowing bakes: the recipes

mind-blowing bakes

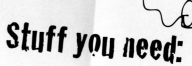

Stuff you need:

100g unsalted butter
125g light soft brown sugar
1 medium egg
1½ tsp vanilla extract
½ tsp baking powder
175g plain flour
50ml buttermilk
1 tbsp red cochineal food colouring
75g cream cheese
225g icing sugar, plus extra
for dusting

Makes 13 pies

HOT
GOODS!

These bright red little treats are made with a natural red food colouring and buttermilk – a secret ingredient that makes your cakes deliciously soft – just like velvet!

Step 1

Preheat the oven to 180°C/fan 160°C/gas mark 4. Line two baking sheets with baking paper. Draw round a 5cm plain cookie cutter to mark out 26 light pencil circles on the baking paper. Turn the paper over.

CRIMSON VELVET WHOOPIE PIES!

Step 2

Beat together 75g butter and all the sugar until pale and fluffy. Add the egg and 1 tsp vanilla extract. Beat again until smooth. Add the baking powder, flour, buttermilk and colouring. Whisk for 1 minute only, until well combined .

Step 3

Drop teaspoonfuls of the cake mixture onto the drawn-out circles and spread until it just fills them. Bake for 12-15 minutes. After 10 minutes cooling, transfer to a wire rack to cool completely.

Step 4

Beat the remaining butter with the cream cheese, remaining vanilla extract and icing sugar. Sandwich the red cakes together with the creamy filling. Dust with icing sugar. Delicious!

The Science Bit

Is cochineal really made from beetles?

Well, yes and no. The stuff we call cochineal is a chemical extract of carminic acid made from the bodies of crushed female scale insects from South and Central America! But they are not beetles. Don't let this put you off cochineal though. This red pigment has been used for centuries by the Aztecs and native Americans!

CHOCCY CHOUX PUFFS

Stuff you need:

75g unsalted butter
60g strong plain flour
2 large eggs, beaten
300ml double cream
1 tbsp icing sugar
75g dark chocolate
75g white chocolate

Makes 8

HOT GOODS!

Choux is pronounced like 'shoe' but is as light and fluffy as a cloud! So how are these so scrumptiously yummy AND so perfectly puffy?

Step 1

Preheat the oven to 200°C/fan 180°C/gas mark 6. Place 50g of butter into a pan and add 150ml water. Heat until the butter melts, then turn up the heat until the water boils. Remove the pan from the heat and add all the flour. Beat with a wooden spoon until the mixture forms a soft ball in the centre of the pan. Allow to cool.

Step 2

Whisk the beaten eggs, a spoonful at a time, into the cooled mixture until smooth. Place evenly spaced spoonfuls of mixture onto two wet baking sheets. Bake for 10 minutes, then increase the oven temperature to 220°C/fan 200°C/gas mark 7. Bake for a further 15 minutes. Remove from the oven and transfer to a wire rack. Make a slit in the sides of the buns to allow the steam to escape.

Step 3

Whip the cream until thick and stir in the icing sugar. Spoon into the split buns.

The Science Bit

What makes choux pastry so puffy?

Choux has a high water content and when it is baked in the oven, the water evaporates to form steam. But that steam cannot escape because the protein in the eggs binds the outside of the dough 'balloon' so that it remains puffy once you have let the air escape from the slit!

Step 4

Roughly chop the white and dark chocolate. Melt each in separate bowls over a pan of hot water, with half of the remaining butter added to each bowl. Allow to cool for 10 minutes before dipping the buns in the melted chocolate. Sprinkle with flaked chocolate to decorate!

EXPLODING CUPCAKES!

Popping candy is a cracking good topping to sprinkle on your cupcakes! But where does popping candy get its big bang?

Stuff you need:

For the cupcakes:
150g unsalted butter
150g caster sugar
175g self-raising flour
3 medium eggs
1 tsp vanilla extract

For the frosting:
300g unsalted butter
500g icing sugar
1½ tsp vanilla extract
Food colourings

To decorate:
Popping candy
Edible glitter sprinkles

Makes 18 cupcakes

HOT GOODS!

Step 1

Preheat the oven to 180°C/fan 160°C /gas mark 4. Line two bun tins with paper cases. Place all the cupcake ingredients into a bowl and whisk for 2 minutes.

Step 2

Divide the mixture evenly between the cases. Bake for 18–20 minutes until golden. Transfer to a wire rack to cool.

Step 3

For the frosting, beat the butter and icing sugar until smooth. Add the vanilla and 2-3 tbsp hot water and beat again. Divide the mixture into bowls and add a few drops of food colouring to each bowl.

Step 4

Use a piping bag to add swirls of frosting on to your cupcakes. Sprinkle with popping candy and edible glitter. Eat straight away for cakes that are sure to be a blast!

The Science Bit

What gives popping candy its big bang?

Popping candy is made like other hard candy, except that carbon dioxide (CO_2) is added at high pressure when the mixture of sugar, lactose, corn syrup and flavourings have been heated to boiling point. The CO_2 stays 'trapped' in bubbles, with walls that harden as the candy cools. When the candy hits your tongue and melts, the high-pressure CO_2 escapes with a loud 'pop'!

An egg is a giant single cell, just like the cells that make up your body!

The Science Bit

How does custard change from a liquid to a solid?

The process of changing a liquid protein (the custard) to a solid (the set custard filling) is called coagulation, and this is done by heating. Custard is a mixture of eggs, milk and sugar. When heated, the protein in the eggs and milk coagulate to change the texture of the food.

SQUIDGY WIDGY CUSTARD TARTS

Crisp on the outside and squidgy on the inside – these custard tarts are irresistible. One will not be enough!

Step 1

Preheat the oven to 190°C/ fan 170°C/gas mark 5. Roll out the pastry on a floured surface to 1cm thick and 30 x 40cm in area. Cut out 10 circles of about 10cm diameter. Use them to line a muffin tin.

Step 2

Whisk together the custard, vanilla, lemon rind and eggs and pour into the pastry cases. Bake for 35–40 minutes until the filling is set. Allow to cool completely before transferring them to a baking tray.

Step 3

Dust the tarts thickly with icing sugar and grill under a high heat for 2 minutes or until the sugar starts to brown and caramelize.

OOZING CRUST PIZZA

This pizza features stretchy mozzarella cheese as a topping but also as a filling for the pizza crust. Cheese-o-rama!

Stuff you need:

145g pizza base mix
1 tbsp flour, for dusting
1 ball mozzarella cheese, diced
2 tbsp sun dried tomato paste
4 cherry plum tomatoes, halved
Handful fresh basil leaves

Serves 2

HOT GOODS!

Step 1

Preheat the oven to 220°C/ fan 200°C/gas mark 7. Make the pizza base mix according to the instructions.

Knead the dough on a lightly floured surface until smooth and elastic. Press out into a 25cm circle.

Step 2

Arrange half the mozzarella around the dough edge in a circle about 1cm in. Wet the edge of the dough and gently lift it over the cheese. Press down to enclose it all the way around. Allow the dough to prove in a warm place for 15 minutes.

Step 3

Spread the tomato paste over the pizza base and add the remaining mozzarella, cherry tomatoes and basil leaves over the top. Bake for **12-15** minutes until the cheese has melted.

As you hEAT MOZZAReLLA thE pROtEins uncoil AnD bEcomE stRingy AnD ELAStic!

The Science Bit

Cheese gives you nightmares: science fact or urban myth?

If you go to bed with a full stomach, you may spend more of the night in REM (rapid eye movement) sleep, which is when your most vivid dreams occur. But there is no evidence to suggest that cheese causes your dreams to be bad.
Conclusion: URBAN MYTH!

VERY BERRY CHOCO RIPPLE MERINGUES

These snowy peaks of magic are made from a combination of everyday ingredients. Crisp on the outside and chewy on the inside, the texture is simply irresistible!

Stuff you need:

3 egg whites
175g caster sugar
2 tbsp cocoa powder
300ml whipped cream
Mixed fresh berries

Makes 6

Step 1

Preheat the oven to 120°C/fan 100°C/gas mark 1/2. Whisk the egg whites with an electric hand whisk until just stiff. You should be able to hold the bowl over your head without any falling out! While whisking, add the sugar a spoonful at a time until the meringue becomes thick and glossy.

Step 2

Sift the cocoa powder over the meringue and fold in with a metal spoon to achieve a 'rippled' effect.

Step 3

Line a baking sheet with baking paper and spoon on 6 piles of meringue. Bake for 2 hours. Turn the oven off and leave the meringues in the oven for a further hour. Serve piled with whipped cream and fresh berries!

The Science Bit

Can meringues ever change back into egg whites?

No. When we whisk egg whites we are breaking down the protein chains in the structure of the egg white. This process is called 'denaturing'. As the denaturing of protein cannot be reversed, this process is known as an irreversible change. So, meringues, listen up! You will never be egg whites again!

KITCHEN SINK POT PIES

Everything-but-the-kitchen-sink can be thrown in to these yummy pot pies to really get your tastebuds a-jangling!

Step 1

Whizz the flour and butter in a food processor until the mixture resembles fine breadcrumbs. Add **4-5** tbsp water until the mixture forms a pastry. Allow to chill for 30 minutes.

Step 2

Preheat the oven to 200°C/fan 180°C/gas mark 6. Roll out two-thirds of the pastry and use a **10cm** cutter to stamp out 9 circles to line a muffin tin.

Step 3

Fry the bacon, chicken and thyme over a medium heat for 7-8 minutes, stirring occasionally until cooked through. Stir in the cheese and apple sauce. Spoon the mixture into pastry cases.

The Science Bit

What is 'umami'?

Umami is one of the 5 flavours (including salt, sweet, sour and bitter) that human beings can detect through receptor cells on their tongues. The word 'umami' was first used by a Japanese professor who discovered that various foods contained this savoury, meaty flavour. Foods with a high umami content are red meats, fish such as anchovies, sardines and tuna, seafood, soy sauce, tomatoes and cheese.

Step 4

Roll out the remaining pastry and stamp out 9 x 8-cm circles. Wet the edges of the circles and press them down firmly onto the filled pastry cases. Brush the pie tops with beaten egg and season with salt and pepper. Bake for 25-30 minutes until golden. Allow to cool in the tin for 10-15 minutes before tucking in!

73

HOT ICE CREAM SPARKLE

How can you bake ice cream in a hot oven without it melting? Make this amazing hot-but-cold dessert, then serve it to your friends!

The Science Bit

How can you bake ice cream without it melting?

When we whisk up meringue we make loads of little pockets of air in the mixture! When the meringue is spooned over the ice cream all those nifty air pockets acts as insulators which prevent warm air from getting inside and melting the ice cream! The heat from the oven also starts to caramelize the sugar in the meringue and forms a delicious golden brown crust on the outside, which forms a protective layer over the ice cream, too. Bingo!

Step 1

Halve the muffins horizontally and place the 4 pieces equally spaced onto a baking sheet. Pile a quarter of the ice cream over each muffin and place in the freezer until ready to use. Preheat the oven to 230°C/fan 210°C/gas mark 8.

Step 2

Whisk the egg whites with an electric hand whisk until they are stiff and will stay in the bowl when it is upturned! While whisking, add the sugar a spoonful at a time. The meringue will become white, thick and glossy.

Step 3

Cover the muffins and ice cream with the meringue, working quickly before the ice cream melts. Ensure you 'fill in' any holes that will allow heat in to melt the ice cream. Bake immediately for 3-4 minutes until golden brown. Sprinkle with edible glitter and serve.

SUPER SEEDY FLOWERPOT BREAD

You don't even need to be a green-fingered gardener to watch these delicious mini flowerpot loaves grow. All you need to do is awaken the yeast!

Step 1

Preheat the oven to 220°C/fan 200°C/gas mark 7. Wash the pots in hot soapy water. Rinse and pat dry. Brush them inside and out with oil and place on a baking tray. Bake for 10 minutes. Very carefully remove from the oven and allow to cool completely. Turn off the oven.

Stuff you need:

- 6 small, new terracotta flowerpots
- 4 tbsp vegetable oil
- 15g softened butter
- 15g sesame seeds
- 15g poppy seeds
- 25g pumpkin seeds
- 25g sunflower seeds
- 1 tbsp black treacle
- 1 sachet (7g) fast-action dried yeast
- 500g wholemeal bread flour
- 2 tbsp milk

Makes 6 bread pots

HOT GOODS!

Step 2

Brush the insides of the pots with softened butter. Mix all the seeds together and sprinkle half onto the buttery insides. Tip upside down and save any seeds that do not stick.

Step 3

Mix the treacle with **100ml** warm water. Stir in the yeast and allow to sit for 5 minutes to 'foam'. Sift the flour into a bowl and stir in the yeast mixture. Add **400ml** warm water and half the remaining seeds. Use your hands to form a soft dough.

Step 4

Knead the dough for 3-4 minutes until smooth. Divide into 6 balls and place into the pots. Brush with milk and scatter over any remaining seeds. Leave the pots to prove in a warm place for 30 minutes until the dough doubles in size. Preheat the oven to 230°C/fan 210°C/ gas mark 8. Bake the pots on a baking tray for 15 -20 minutes. Serve warm or cold.

The Science Bit

Is yeast really a living organism?

Yes it is! Yeast is actually lots of tiny microscopic fungi (mushroom relatives) that are activated by warmth, moisture and sugar. When we leave dough to prove or rise in a warm place, the yeast in the dough converts natural sugars from the flour into gases which are trapped in the bread. These gases are responsible for all the little holes you can see in a slice of bread, and which create pockets for your jam or peanut butter!

STACK 'EM HIGH CHEESY PUFF PIE

What turns a thick cheese sauce into a deliciously light and airy souffle when baked? Read on...

Stuff you need:

75g unsalted butter
25g fine fresh white breadcrumbs
40g plain flour
1/2 tsp English mustard powder
300ml whole milk
100g mature Cheddar cheese, grated
4 large eggs, separated

Serves 6

HOT GOODS!

Step 1

Preheat a baking tray in 200°C/fan 180°C/ gas mark 6. Melt 25g of the butter and use it to brush the insides of six 250ml ramekins. Sprinkle with the fine breadcrumbs to coat and set aside.

Step 2

Melt the remaining butter in a saucepan. Add the flour and mustard powder and stir for 1 minute over a low heat. Gradually add the milk and stir until the sauce thickens. Remove from the heat and stir in the cheese and egg yolks. Beat well.

Step 3

Use an electric hand whisk to beat the egg whites until stiff. Stir a large spoonful of whites into the cheese sauce to 'loosen' the mixture. Using a metal spoon gently fold the remaining whites into the sauce. Spoon into the ramekins, filling just to the rim. Clean the ramekin rims with kitchen paper to allow the souffle to rise evenly.

Step 4

Carefully remove the hot baking sheet from the oven and place the ramekins onto it. Bake the mini souffles for 8-10 minutes, until golden. Serve and eat immediately.

The Science Bit

What makes souffle so light and airy?

Air is the most important ingredient in a souffle and is the reason why it rises! When the egg whites are folded into the cheese sauce the fats in the sauce coat the air bubbles in the whites. When heat is applied the air inside the egg whites expands and 'inflates' it. But eat it quickly, because as soon as the air inside is lost the souffle will deflate!

Stuff you need:

15g butter, melted
3 medium eggs
75g caster sugar
125g plain flour
1 tsp easy-blend yeast
50ml warm milk
125g blueberries
150g blackberries
2 tbsp icing sugar

Makes 12

HOT GOODS!

BLUEBERRIES ARE Full of ANTI-oxidANTS which help to combaT AND EliMiNATE ToxiNS iN oUR bodiES

The Science Bit

Why are blueberries so super?

These little purple berries really are a powerhouse of good stuff! One of the top 10 superfoods ever, they are high in vitamin C, anti-oxidants and fibre, all of which are excellent for keeping your skin in good condition as well as fighting diseases like cancer, heart disease and asthma. Scientists also say that blueberries keep your brain more active.

BLACK & BLUE BUNS

Don't be fooled by the name of these buns. They are totally and utterly good for you as they contain an amazingly talented superfood...

Step 1

Preheat the oven to 220°C/fan 200°C/gas mark 7. Brush a 12-hole bun tin with melted butter.

Step 2

Whisk together the eggs, sugar and flour until smooth. Mix the yeast and warm milk together until smooth and whisk into the egg mixture. Pour evenly into the prepared bun tin.

Step 3

Scatter the blueberries and blackberries into the centre of each bun. Bake for 12-15 minutes until golden brown. Dust with the icing sugar to serve.

Stuff you need:

175g unsalted butter
200g golden caster sugar
1 medium egg
1 tsp vanilla extract
400g plain flour, plus extra
for dusting
32 plain boiled sweets

Makes 32 cookies

HOT GOODS!

HUMAN bEiNGS ARE 'PROGRAMMED' through Evolution to Enjoy sWEEt foods!

Stained glass candy in a cookie, all rolled into one – it's magic!

Step 1

Preheat the oven to 180°C/fan 160°C/gas mark 4. Line two baking trays with baking paper. Cream the butter and sugar until pale. Stir in the egg and vanilla extract. Fold in the flour, and add 1–2 tbsp water to form a dough. Wrap the dough in cling film and chill for 30 minutes.

STAINED GLASS COOKIES

Step 2

Unwrap the dough and cut in half. On a floured surface, roll half of the dough to a 3mm thickness. Using 10cm cookie cutters cut shapes from the dough and place on the baking sheets. Repeat with the remaining dough.

Step 3

Use a 3cm cutter to stamp circles from the centre of your cookies and put a boiled sweet into the hole. Bake for 10 minutes. Tilt the tray to allow the melted sweets to fill the holes. Cool for 5 minutes, then transfer to a wire rack to cool completely.

The Science Bit

Are boiled sweets <u>really</u> boiled?

Yes! A boiled sweet is a concentrated sugar solution. As sugar and water are heated, the water boils away and the sugar concentrates as the temperature of the mixture rises. The highest temperature and most concentrated sugar solution results in boiled sweets, which become hard

fascinating fruits: the recipes

fascinating fruits

TROPICAL FRUIT WITH GOO-EY CHOCOLATE DIP

Rich with choccy-ness this dip is the perfect complement to fresh and tangy tropical fruits. But what makes the dip stay goo-ey enough for you and your pals to keep coming back for more (and more)?

Step 1

Soak 12 wooden skewers in water for 25 minutes, to stop them burning when they go under a hot grill.

Step 2

Peel the kiwi fruit and pineapple and cut into chunks. De-hull the strawberries. Slice the star fruit and brush with lemon juice. Cut a slice from either side of the mango and discard the stone. Cut a criss-cross pattern into the flesh, turn inside out and cut away the mango cubes.

Stuff you need:

2 kiwi fruit
1/4 fresh pineapple
8 strawberries
1 star fruit
1 tbsp lemon juice
1 large ripe mango
Juice of 1/2 lemon
8 tbsp runny honey
8 tbsp milk
8 tbsp double cream
225g dark chocolate, broken into squares

Serves 4

HOT GOODS!

86

Step 3

Thread the fruit onto the pointed end of each skewer.

THE STAR FRUIT IS AN EXCELLENT SOURCE OF ASCORBIC ACID (VITAMIN C), IMPORTANT IN KEEPING BONES, TEETH AND SKIN HEALTHY!

The Science Bit

What makes the chocolate stay runny?

Melted chocolate usually sets, agreed? It's an example of a reversible change because chocolate melts, sets solid, then melts again. But here, double cream, honey and milk are added. The fats in the cream and milk combine with the cocoa butter, a vegetable fat in the chocolate. This combo of fats can produce a (WARNING: science word coming up!) eutectic system, which, in simple terms, means the chocolate stays runny!

Step 4

Put the honey, milk, double cream and chocolate in a small saucepan and heat gently over a low heat, stirring continuously until melted. Pour into a small bowl and serve with the fruit skewers.

INCREDIBLE EDIBLE TIE-DYE ICES

Who said you can only tie-dye clothes? Why not try lollies instead! They are packed full of juicy blackberries all wrapped up in a creamy 'brain-freezing' yoghurt!

Stuff you need:

85g fresh blackberries
Finely grated rind and juice of 1 lemon
4 tbsp icing sugar
300ml vanilla or natural yoghurt

Makes 4 lollies

Step 1

Place the blackberries and 1 tbsp lemon juice into a bowl and mash with a fork.

Step 2

Mix together the remaining lemon juice, lemon rind icing sugar and yoghurt.

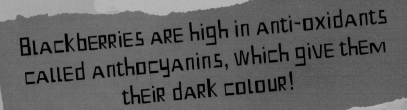

BLACKBERRIES ARE high in Anti-oxidants called anthocyanins, which give them their dark colour!

Step 3

Drop a few spoonfuls of yoghurt mixture into 4 x 100ml ice lolly moulds, then add a spoonful of blackberry mixture. Keep doing this until you have used up all the mixture and filled all the moulds.

Step 4

Push a wooden skewer into each lolly mould to stir up the mixtures a little. Cover the lolly moulds with their lids and freeze for at least 12 hours or overnight.

The Science Bit

What exactly is brain freeze?

Brain freeze is the pain you feel when you eat freezing cold food such as an ice cream. When cold food touches the roof of your mouth it makes the blood vessels shrink or constrict. The sharp pain that you can get is caused by the blood rushing back into the blood vessels in order to heat the blood up again. Luckily, brain freeze usually lasts only about 30 seconds!

ICY WATERMELON FRUIT SLICES

There's nothing more refreshing than a slice of watermelon on a hot summer's day. So why not try our icy watermelon sorbet version!

Stuff you need:

1 small watermelon, halved
75g caster sugar
1 medium egg white
75g blueberries

Serves 8

Step 1

Scoop out the flesh from the watermelon halves leaving the shell intact. Roughly chop the flesh.

Step 2

Place the watermelon and sugar into a food processor and whizz to a slushy puree. Pour into a freezer-proof container and freeze for **4** hours until semi-frozen.

The Science Bit

Why add egg whites to sorbet?

Adding egg white to your sorbet help to give it a more creamy consistency and adds volume and texture. It also helps to stabilize the mixture (as an emulsifier). Emulsifying the mixture means that you can keep it in the freezer for longer!

Step 3

Use a fork to break up any large ice crystals. Whisk the egg white until stiff and fold into the frozen mixture. Add the blueberries. Spoon the semi-frozen mixture into one half of the watermelon shell. Cover with clingfilm and freeze overnight. Remove from the freezer 20 minutes before serving.

Stuff you need:

12 bamboo skewers
1 ripe pineapple, peeled
25g butter
25g light muscovado sugar
Finely grated rind of 1 lime
Chopped pistachio nuts

Makes 12

HOT GOODS!

Speed up the ripening of a pineapple by standing it upside down on its leafy end!

Sticky and really juicy, these caramelized hot 'lollies' are even tastier when dipped in chopped pistachios!

Step 1

Soak the skewers in cold water for 25 minutes to stop them burning under the grill. Halve the pineapple lengthways and then cut each half into six long, thin wedges. Push each piece of pineapple onto a wooden skewer.

HOT PINEAPPLE 'LOLLIES'

Step 2

Mix the butter, sugar and lime rind together to make a smooth paste.

Step 3

Heat a griddle pan until smoking and add the pineapple skewers. Cook for 2 minutes on each side until slightly charred. Dot the pineapple with the butter mixture and cook for a further minute until the sugar mixture has dissolved.

Step 4

Sprinkle with pistachio nuts if liked and serve warm.

The Science Bit

Why is pineapple a jelly's worst enemy?

While pineapple is a deliciously nutritious fruit packed with vitamin C and fibre, it also contains an enzyme called bromelain, which acts to digest protein. So, if you add pineapple to a fruit jelly it simply won't set because the bromelain will act on the gelatine proteins and break them down!

SUPER BLUEBERRY CHEESECAKE

One slice will not be enough! Crisp on the bottom, refreshing and creamy in the middle and super fruity on the top. Triple wow!

Stuff you need:

150g coconut biscuits
85g butter
225g caster sugar
Finely grated rind and juice of 2 limes
500g low fat soft curd cheese or quark
300ml double cream
1 x 7g sachet powdered gelatine
250g fresh blueberries

Serves 8

HOT GOODS!

Step 1

Break up the biscuits and whizz in a food processor to make fine crumbs. Melt the butter in a saucepan and stir in the crumbs to coat evenly. Line the base of a 23cm springform cake tin with greaseproof paper. Press the biscuit mixture firmly into the base of the tin. Chill for 10 minutes in the fridge.

Step 2

In a large bowl mix together 150g of the caster sugar, lime zest and half the lime juice, curd cheese and double cream until well combined.

94

Step 3

Sprinkle the gelatine over 3 tbsp of warm water in a small bowl. Leave for 5 minutes. Place the bowl over a pan of hot water and heat until the gelatine has dissolved. Allow to cool for 5 minutes.

Step 4

Drizzle the dissolved gelatine into the creamy cheese mixture and whisk. Pour over the biscuit base and chill for 2-3 hours until set.

Step 5

Place the remaining sugar, lime juice and blueberries into a saucepan and heat gently until the sugar has dissolved and the blueberries are just releasing their juice. Remove the cheesecake from its tin and pour over the blueberry sauce to serve.

 The Science Bit

Why do we add lime?

Lime adds a sharp citrus flavour and its acidity is a good partner to a rich, creamy cheesecake. Plus, scientists believe that our taste buds sense some flavours more strongly if they are offset by other flavours. So, we appreciate the cheesecake even more because it is combined with sour lime!

WOBBLY STRAWBERRY MOUSSE

What is packed full of sweet and nutritious strawberries but is high on the wobble factor? It's our amazing strawberry mousse! Move over jelly...

Step 1

Brush the inside of a 600ml jelly mould with oil. Place the gelatine leaves in a bowl and pour over 150ml cold water. Leave to stand for 5 minutes.

Stuff you need:

1 tsp vegetable oil
5 gelatine leaves
600g strawberries, hulled and quartered
150g icing sugar
450ml double cream
Fresh strawberries and mint leaves, to decorate

Serves 6-8

Did you know? THERE ARE ABOUT 200 SEEDS IN EVERY STRAWBERRY!

Step 2

Place the strawberries and icing sugar into a food processor and whizz to a smooth puree. Sieve the strawberry mixture into a large bowl to create a smooth sauce.

Step 3

Gently warm the cream in a saucepan. Drain the gelatine and add the softened leaves to the cream. Stir until dissolved. Whisk in the strawberry puree, then pour into the jelly mould. Chill overnight.

The Science Bit

What creates the wobble factor?

It's gelatine! When heated gelatine becomes soluble, but when cooled it forms a gel. This gel acts as a kind of protein 'mesh' that traps water from the other liquids present in the recipe. This is a reversible process, as the gelatine will melt on heating but when cooled will reform again.

Step 4

Dip the sides of the jelly mould into a bowl of warm water for about 30 seconds. Lift out of the water and cover with a plate. Turn the mould and the plate over and lift the mould away from the pudding. Decorate with fresh strawberries and mint.

'MAGIC' APPLE & BLACKBERRY PUDDING

Try this fabulously fruity pudding with a delicious sauce that appears - as if by magic!

Step 1

Preheat the oven to 190°C/fan 170°C/gas mark 5. Put the apples and blackberries into an ovenproof dish and sprinkle with 50g of the sugar.

Stuff you need:

450g cooking apples, peeled, and cut into thick slices
225g blackberries
150g caster sugar
25g softened butter
25g plain flour
Finely grated rind and juice of 1 lemon
2 medium eggs, separated
150ml milk
25g flaked almonds
Icing sugar, to dust

Serves 6

HOT GOODS!

Step 2

Cream the butter and remaining sugar until pale and fluffy. Stir in the flour, lemon rind and juice, egg yolks and milk and beat until smooth. Don't worry if your mixture looks curdled!

Step 3

Whisk the egg whites until stiff and fold them into the lemon mixture. Spoon over the fruit to cover. Sprinkle over the flaked almonds.

Step 4

Place the ovenproof dish into a large roasting tin and very carefully pour boiling water until it reaches halfway up the sides of the ovenproof dish. Transfer to the oven and bake for 45–50 minutes. Dust with icing sugar and serve warm.

The Science Bit

What causes the 'magic' sauce?

The magic sauce is the result of the ingredients being denatured (or changed) in a chemical reaction. It's the acid in the lemon juice that helps them change in different ways. The proteins in the eggs and milk break down and release air (causing the pudding mixture to rise) but the cell walls of the fruits break down, making them more liquid. And that's magic!

Stuff you need:

For the ice bowl:
Small handful blueberries
1 kiwi fruit, sliced
1 star fruit, sliced
4 Gerbera flower heads
8 strawberries, halved
Handful ice cubes

For the fruit salad:
1 star fruit
1 lemon, halved
½ small melon, cut into chunks
125g seedless red grapes
1 kiwi fruit, peeled and chopped
300g tinned mandarin oranges
1 small papaya, peeled and chopped
100ml white grape juice

Serves 4-6

Pop on your gloves to make this wonderful icy creation to hold a tasty fruit salad. Brrrr...!

The Science Bit

What is dry ice?

Dry ice is NOT used in this recipe but it is still fascinating to know about! Dry ice is frozen carbon dioxide (CO_2) and is often used to preserve perishable items such a fruit. Fruits frozen with dry ice will

ICE BOWL FRUIT SALAD

Step 1

For the ice bowl, fill a 2.4-litre glass mixing bowl two-thirds full with water. Place a 1.2-litre glass mixing bowl into the centre of the water. Secure with sticky tape so that the smaller bowl is central and the rims are level. Push the fruit and flowers into the water. Add ice cubes to keep them submerged. Freeze overnight.

Step 2

For the fruit salad, carefully slice the star fruit and squeeze over the lemon juice. Combine the melon, grapes, kiwi and oranges with the papaya, star fruit and grape juice. Chill until ready to use.

Step 3

Remove the bowls from the freezer. Fill the smaller one with warm water to and ease it out. Turn the bowl over. Pour warm water over the back of the larger bowl until the ice bowl inside releases. Place it onto a serving plate, add the fruit salad and serve!

NICEY SLICEY SUMMER FRUIT JELLY

This summer jelly is jam-packed with fruity goodness. You will be well on your way to your 5 a-day!

Stuff you need:

75g caster sugar
250ml clear fresh apple and raspberry juice
3 tbsp lemon juice
5 gelatine leaves
2 nectarines, chopped
225g raspberries
225g redcurrants

Serves 6

HOT GOODS!

Step 1

Add 250ml water to the sugar and heat gently in a pan, stirring until the sugar dissolves. Bring to a boil and boil rapidly for 1 minute. Add the apple and raspberry, and the lemon juices.

Raspberries come in many colours. There are black, purple and even golden raspberries!

Step 2

Soften the gelatine in 150ml cold water. Leave for 2-3 minutes. Stand the bowl over a pan of simmering water for 2-3 minutes until the gelatine dissolves. Then add the gelatine to the juice mixture and stir.

Step 3

Place the nectarines, raspberries and redcurrants into a 1.2-litre nonstick loaf tin and mix gently. Pour over the gelatine mixture to cover and allow to set overnight.

Step 4

To release the jelly from the loaf tin, carefully dip the tin into warm water for 30 seconds. Position a plate over the top of the jelly and quickly turn the plate over. Lift the loaf tin off. Ta-dah!

Stuff you need:

500ml full fat milk
25g dried milk powder
3 tbsp 'live' natural yoghurt
85g dried apricots, halved
50g raisins
50g dried cherries
1 fruit teabag
1 split vanilla pod
1 red apple, cored and sliced
Runny honey, to serve

Serves 4

HOT GOODS!

Did you know that some yoghurt is a living culture? Why not try making our homemade yoghurt recipe for a totally wholesome breakfast?

Step 1

Place the milk and milk powder into a saucepan and whisk until well combined. Place over the lowest heat and allow to warm gently without boiling.

HOMEMADE YOGHURT WITH FRUIT SQUISH

Step 2

Stir in the yoghurt and pour into a flask. Set aside and leave overnight until set.

Step 3

Place the fruit into a pan with the teabag, vanilla pod and 150ml boiling water and leave to go cold.

Step 4

Drain the fruit, discard the teabag and remove the vanilla pod. Very carefully remove the seeds from the pod and stir into the yoghurt. Divide the yoghurt between 4 glasses. Spoon over the soaked fruit and add apple slices. Drizzle with honey to serve.

The Science Bit

How is yoghurt a 'living culture'?

Milk (the main ingredient of yoghurt) contains a natural sugar, lactose. Naturally occurring bacteria feed off lactose and produce lactic acid. When bacteria have warmth (such as in the flask) they breed and multiply, producing more lactic acid. Lactic acid changes the texture and taste of the milk by a process called denaturing. Hey presto! We have yoghurt.

Stuff you need:

500g bag frozen mixed summer fruits
400g Greek yoghurt
Finely grated rind and juice of 1 large orange
2 tbsp icing sugar
Small handful fresh cherries
Mint sprigs, to decorate

Serves 6

CHERRIES ARE RICH IN MELATONIN WHICH HAS A SOOTHING AND RELAXING EFFECT ON THE BRAIN!

The Science Bit

Does freezing alter your fresh fruit?

Fresh fruit retains a lot of its nutrients if frozen quickly after picking. But fresh fruit tends to lose its shape when defrosted. This happens because the cells are broken when the water in them expands as it freezes. So frozen fruits are ideal for cooking or blending into recipes like frozen yoghurt!

INSTANT FROZEN YOGHURT

This ready-before-you-know-it frozen yoghurt is a healthy alternative to ice cream since it contains half the fat and is stuffed full of healthy fruit!

Step 1

Place the frozen fruits, yoghurt, orange rind and juice and icing sugar into a food processor. Whizz up the mixture (using a spatula to scrape down the sides of the food processor) until totally smooth.

Step 2

Spoon the yoghurt mixture into serving glasses. Top with fresh cherries and mint sprigs to serve.

STICKY LICKY BANOFFEE CONES

Whizz up an banana-licious treat in a cone! Bananas are healthy and taste good but they also have other very special uses...

Stuff you need:

4 bananas
4 wafer ice cream cones
2 tbsp dulce de leche (thick caramel sauce)
½ tsp vanilla extract
4 tbsp caster sugar
150ml buttermilk
8 dried banana chips
2 tbsp grated chocolate

Makes 4 cones

Step 1

Peel 3 bananas and cut into thick slices. Arrange on a baking tray and freeze for at least 2 hours until solid.

Step 2

While keeping the bananas frozen, peel and chop the remaining banana and push a quarter of it into each cone. Stand the cones upright in a jug to help you. Add 1 tbsp of caramel sauce into each cone.

Step 3

Remove the bananas from the freezer and whizz up in a food processor with the vanilla, sugar and half the buttermilk. Scrape down the sides using a spatula, add the remaining buttermilk and whizz again until smooth.

The Science Bit

How are bananas useful?

To speed up the ripening of fruits such as avocados, mangoes, peaches and pears, place a ripe banana and the unripe fruit into a paper bag. The banana emits a gas called ethylene which acts a a signal to other fruit to start ripening. How useful is that?

Step 4

Spoon the ice cream into the cones, top with dried banana, a drizzle of caramel sauce and dust with chocolate.

GLOSSARY

ANTI-OXIDANTS substances in foods that repair cells and protect us from disease

ASCORBIC ACID a form of vitamin C, mainly found in fruit and vegetables

BACTERIA tiny living organisms that can grow on food

BAMBOO SKEWERS wooden sticks on which you can thread meat, fish or vegetables for grilling or barbecuing

BEAT a quick and vigorous mix with a spoon or whisk

BICARBONATE OF SODA a soluble white powder mainly used in fizzy drinks and as a raising agent in baking

BLEND to mix two or more ingredients together

BUTTERMILK a slightly sour liquid left after butter has been churned

CARAMELIZE the process of converting sugar to caramel when it is heated

CELLS basic unit of all living things

CITRIC ACID a sharp-tasting acid found in lemons and other citrus fruits

COAGULATION when protein molecules or chains rearrange themselves, break or change

COLLAGEN a protein found in animal tissue. When heated collagen turns to gelatine

CORNFLOUR a white powder that is used to thicken liquids such as soups, stews and gravies

CULTURE the growth of organisms

CUMIN a pungent spice often used in Indian cooking

CURDS when milk is being made into cheese, the solid parts of the cheese are known as curds

DESICCATE to dry a food product

EDIBLE something (usually a food substance) that is fit to be eaten

ELECTRIC HAND WHISK a hand-held mixer with two or three whisks attached

EMULSIFY to create a mixture of two or more liquids, which would not normally mix

ENDORPHINS chemicals that can act on the brain to make us feel happy

ENZYMES molecules found in our food that speed up natural processes

FIBRE a substance found in some foods such as cereals, fruits and vegetables that adds bulk to our diets and aids digestion

FILO PASTRY a wafer-thin pastry

FRY To cook with oil in a shallow frying pan

FUNGHI a group of living things, which includes yeast for making bread and also mushrooms

GELATINE a setting agent used in many puddings and desserts

GRAM FLOUR a flour made from ground chickpeas often used in Indian cooking

GRIDDLE PAN a heavy cast-iron pan that creates 'chargrilled' lines across your food

KERNEL the seed or hard husk of a cereal such as wheat

KNEAD to fold, push and pull dough until it becomes soft and smooth

LACTIC ACID an acid present in our milk and also produced in our muscles when we exercise

MOLECULES the smallest units of a chemical substance or compound

NORI dried sheets of seaweed used in making sushi rolls

NUTRIENTS substances found in food and drink, including carbohydrates, minerals, proteins and vitamins

OXIDATION the reaction that occurs when a food substance is exposed to air

POTASSIUM a mineral found in foods such as avocados, dried apricots and fish, and which is essential in maintaining the nervous system

PRESERVATIVES substances added to food to prevent it from spoiling

PROTEIN the second most common substance in our body (after water), helping us to grow and fight disease

PROVE when a dough is left in a warm place to rise

SEASON to flavour food with salt and pepper

SIEVE to strain a liquid or push something through a sieve to get rid of lumps

SIMMER to cook at just below boiling point, bubbling gently

SOLUBLE substances that can be easily dissolved in a liquid

SPRINGFORM CAKE TIN a cake tin with removable sides and base

SUPERFOODS nutrient-rich foods that can help to fight off ageing and illness

TOSS to lightly throw ingredients together to combine them

TOXINS poisonous substances produced by cells

TURMERIC a bright yellow spice used mainly in Indian and Asian cooking

WHISK to mix something quickly to get air into it

WOK a large, deep frying pan used in Chinese cooking

YEAST an agent used to raise dough in breadmaking

INDEX